Women IN MINISTRY

CHALLENGING CURRENT MINDSETS ABOUT A WOMAN'S ROLE IN LEADERSHIP IN THE CHURCH

ALLEN W. COOK

PRESS

Introduction

The basis for this book goes back to a prophetic word I received back in 1990. My wife and I attended a Pastoral Retreat/Ministry time in Arizona, hosted by Iverna Thompkins. As was her custom, she spent personal time with all of the attendees for that week. As we were out by the pool, I noticed a large palm tree in the corner where we were sitting. I couldn't help but think of Deborah, the Old Testament judge who gave good counsel to the nation in a time of great turmoil. Iverna, is in my estimation, one of the greatest women preachers and teachers I have ever had the privilege of hearing. Her insight into the scriptures is nothing less than profound. She has been a pioneer with passion in the church for many years. I thank God for her sacrifice.

She told me that she saw me with satellite churches out of our church and that she was sure others had said similar things to me (they had). But she said the Lord had shown her something unusual in the scriptures about me. She pointed out the passage in Genesis chapter 29 where Jacob arrives at Paddan Aram. He encounters Shepherds at a local well. However, when his cousin Rachel arrives, he lifts the stone from off the well and helps Rachel water her sheep. She could not lift the stone herself and was dependent upon the other Shepherds for help. Consequently, she was often last. You must make note of the fact that Laban had large flocks so Rachel was not the overseer of a few token sheep. She was a leader. The encouraging word that Iverna gave me was that God would use me to lift the stone off the well so that the sheep may be watered. I would help women (lift the stone so that the sheep could be watered). I cared deeply that the sheep were watered and I realized that this watering could come from a man or a woman. I would help many women fulfill their ministries and callings from the Lord.

Today is the greatest day for women in the church. There are so many in the National Spotlight and many thousands of other women who are changing the world through their gifts and callings.

Since that day with Iverna, God has continually given me wisdom on the women question. I realize that many books have been written about the subject but I am taking the time now to offer my point of view. May you find it refreshing and unconventional?

Excelsior! (ever upward)
Pastor Allen W. Cook

Chapter 1

THE GENESIS

The Bible begins with a book called Genesis. How appropriate since Genesis means birth, creation, or beginning.

God said, "Let us make man in our image, in our likeness, and let them rule over the fish of the sea and the birds of the air, over the livestock, over all the earth and over all the creatures that move along the ground. So God made man (the Adam) in his own image, in the image of God he created him; male and female he created them." Genesis 1:26, 27

We see here in the Garden that male and female were equal. Equal in creation that is, one could and would not exist without the other. There are definite differences, such as strength, stamina, biological make-up, and emotional skills but the two creations in the eyes of God are equal for his purpose. When God said let us make man, the man is a "they," not just a he. The Adam is a male and female, the best translation would be that God made a human, or humanity. By having the one "Adam" represent the two, "male and female" the writer had emphasized the oneness and unity of Adam (humanity) as male and female. So in order for us to understand God's nature we must have male and female.

Notice that God who is one says, "Let us make Adam (humanity) in our image. We can surmise from this verse that both sexes are needed to reflect the true nature of God.

God reiterates again in Genesis 5:1-2 where he documents the history of Adam:

"This is the book of the generations of Adam. In the day that God created man, in the likeness of God made he him: Male and female created he them; and blessed them, and called THEIR name Adam, in the day when they were created."

In Genesis 1:28 God says let them rule over the creation, to be fruitful and to subdue the earth and all living creatures upon it. The word rule (radah) in conjunction with the preposition (over), gives us the evidence that not only are male and female needed to reflect God's image but both are commanded to have rulership and authority. They both share in power and leadership in the relationship that God has ordained for them. Please make note that from the heart of love that God created, he envisioned man as not just male but female as well. One definition of the word woman is "man with a womb". So when God began this whole creation thing, he made sure that we understood that Adam and Eve were called to stand together and rule together. Both sexes have superior traits and both sexes need the strengths of the other. In Genesis 2: we see a more detailed explanation of how God created man. The word used here for Eve is: "help meet". This word has been translated more culturally than Biblically.

> Genesis 2:18 says, "And the Lord God thought it was not good
> for the Adam to be by himself; "I will make for him a helper as
> if in front of him."

He formed the male body from the dust and breathed into his nostrils the breath of life, Genesis 2: 7. As Adam began to tend the garden he noticed that the animals were all in pairs, male and female. This caused Adam, I believe, to desire a companion. God had already anticipated the need and he caused a deep sleep to fall upon him. He took a rib from Adam. This is very significant. God could have taken more dirt and formed the woman or he could have used a bone from anywhere in the body to create the woman. However, he chose his side (a rib) and I believe that this is where women gain equal status in the sight of God. Adam immediately affirms that status when he prophesies and says, "This is now bone of my bone and flesh of my flesh, she shall be called (woman) man with a womb, equal to me yet in function different.

Adam goes on to build the first family with his prophetic words. He, (Adam) is the originator of their destiny, as far as their relationship with each other. God had already decreed that together they would rule the world.

God gave Adam the job of setting the order for their relationship. This order Adam set was again one of equality. First, Adam called for an exclusive relationship. They were to cleave only to each other. The word cleave means to literally "be glued" together. That is stuck together for each other.

Eve was taken out of man, and when he awoke he not only saw his partner but he felt something missing inside of himself. He felt an empty spot perhaps for the first time that needed to be filled and could only be filled by the creation called woman.

Secondly, the two becoming one is where Adam sees them building for God together. I believe that he saw the best in each of them and said we must take that best and build a life that is honoring to God. They as a couple were to live a life that was obedient to the counsel and command of God to take the Garden of Eden and reproduce it through out the earth.

Thirdly, Adam decreed that they would forsake all others for one another. This created in Eve a sense of exclusivity. She was his and no one else's. She felt protected and treasured.

The Genesis story is the very beginning of God's dream for a man and a woman. They were to have an exclusive relationship. It was to be lived in vulnerability. They were both naked and not ashamed. This speaks not only of physical nakedness but I believe emotional and mental disclosure of the most intimate kind. To be naked is to be vulnerable and to have nothing hidden. So the pattern for the relationship is set in the Garden.

No shame, no fear of each other, no one ruling over the other, but a mutual relationship of submission to God and each other. Adam did have the direction for the relationship and I believe because he took his role seriously and decreed the best for Eve, who happily deferred and referred to him often as they worked together to be fruitful, and multiply and fill the earth with the will of God.

For now, we see a couple that is under mutual submission to God and one another: (Paul instructs the believers in the church as Ephesus to live the same model), as they are to fill the earth and reproduce mankind and the environment that God gave them in the garden.

After the fall the relationship changed drastically.

God now tells the woman that she will desire to rule over her husband instead of work with him. God says, your desire shall be to your husband Eve would from henceforth, have difficulty trusting and letting Adam lead the relationship as he had previously decreed it. They would forever wrestle over words and desire to control each other instead of letting God control them and everything around them as they submitted to Him. They no longer viewed each other as equal partners but separate rulers, capable of living without each other, at least emotionally. It was a sad day for us all!

Chapter 2

THREE MATRIARCHS

EVE the MOTHER

Eve being the first woman in creation and first mentioned in the scriptures, was a ruler and as her name implies, a giver of life. We often do not think of her like that but God told both of them to multiply and rule over the earth. She co-leads with her husband in fulfilling God's mandate to reproduce and multiply and rule the earth. There is no indication in the Genesis account that Eve was inferior, or that she was somehow less capable of farming (their first occupation), or controlling the animals and nature. In fact, if you look at what is written it appears they had a dream marriage. Both ruled and reigned under the Lordship of God Elohim. Each brought to their calling, their unique gifting and there by honoring and pleasing God. It must have been truly grand! Eve was a ruler, no more or no less than Adam. Genesis sets the foundation for what God builds upon. He shows us clearly that women are included in his plan as leaders and rulers.

After the fall the leadership role is subverted and the curse now upon them is not the sense of unity they enjoyed but a comparison and competition. Eve will now desire to RULE her husband instead of REIGN with him.

> Genesis 3:16 Unto the woman God said, "I will greatly multiply your sorrow and your conception; in sorrow you shall bring forth children; and your desire shall be to your husband and he shall rule over you."

At this moment Adam, the man, takes the leadership role in a new way than before the fall. Some translators believe that this says you will desire to rule your husband, other translator's say you will now be subject to your husband and consult him. Both of these interpretations imply that the previous state of leadership by Eve has now been subjected to a lower status. The fall has brought disunity if you will, and now there is a COMPETITION instead of a COMPLETING.

The good news is that Christ has redeemed us from the cursing produced by the fall. If we are to truly benefit from the work of Christ we must take a fresh look at old patterns of interpretation in regards to women in ministry. Christ redemption is complete and perfect. His work on the cross was an act by God to restore spiritual order in the cosmos where the angelic host dwell but also to restore the earth to His original purpose. With those thoughts in mind we should reflect upon the role of women in the church and see if we are operating pre-curse or post-curse in the church?

Paul says in Galatians 3:26-29, "You are all sons of God through faith in Christ Jesus, for all of you who were baptized into Christ have clothed yourselves with Christ. There is neither Jew nor Greek, slave nor free, male nor female, for you are all one in Christ Jesus. If you belong to Christ then you are Abraham's seed and heirs according to the promise."

He is of course speaking of our spiritual state, and our spiritual state in God is not based totally in what our sex is. I do not believe he is trying to create a sexual identity crisis but I do believe he is placing the emphasis of our relationship with Christ where it should be, in the finished work of what Jesus has done and that work can operate through a female body as well as a man.

SARAI the PRINCESS

Also we must make note of Sarai, Abraham's wife. God changed her name to Sarah meaning (Princess) because she was destined to be the progenitor of a great nation of Kings and Priest.

Name changes in the Bible are extremely significant. God changed Abram to Abraham, interjecting his own breath once again into the human race. Jacob's name was changed to Israel because of his destiny for the promised seed of Genesis. Name changes in the Bible are usually the result of a shift in the person towards their destiny in God.

Sarah again affirms to us that she was honored by God as a ruler by fulfilling her divine and natural calling, to bear a child. Prince's and Princess' reflect ruler ship. Sarah was equally important when God made his promise to

Abraham to make of him a great nation and give him a natural born son of his own loins. God considered them equal. He (God) honored Sarah's request to banish Haggar over Abraham's counsel. Perhaps Sarah had a better picture of the future in this area than Abraham.

Given the intuitive nature of women, they can see things in regards to family that men often miss. This should not create a feeling or sense of superiority in the women and neither should it create spiritual inferiority in the man. I have been wearied over the years as I have heard so many men play down their spirituality. We must remember that seeing in the spirit is not a gender gift, restricted to one or the other. Seeing in the spirit is a part of our spiritual DNA from God. All things are naked and open before him and as he chooses he allows us to see a part of what he sees. This should not produce posturing in men or perching in women.

Sarah was privileged to set the order for the first household of faith by seeing that Issac and Ishmael could not co-exist in the same household. Just as today our flesh cannot coexist and lead in the household of faith. We must surrender the self made ideas of man and the attempts to build God's kingdom apart from God's promises and through faith. Sarah led the way in making the decision to expel Haggar. Abraham and Sarah both had a moment of failure in looking to the flesh to fulfill the spiritual promise God gave them. However, Sarah led the way in dealing with this carnal aftermath and God honored her for it as proof in ordering Abraham to listen to his wife's counsel.

RACHEL the SHEPHERDESS

Finally, we see Rachel in a leadership role. She is the Shepherdess of her father's flock. We know that this was no small flock because Laban was a rich and powerful man and wealth in Biblical days was determined mostly by livestock. Of course there was silver and gold but being a nomadic society wealth often came in the form of sheep, goats, and camels. Rachel led her father's flock; again this was mostly a man's job and required great courage and strength.

The fact that her names means compassionate womb describes the spiritual characteristics of a true pastor. He must have compassion on the sheep. Jesus said in Mark 8:2, "I have COMPASSION on the multitude. Paul exhorts us to have compassion one for another.

We often reflect on David the Shepherd King who killed the lion and the bear. Well, Rachel had to protect her father's flock just like David. We have no biblical account of her fending off wolves and other predators. There is no need to state the obvious. She was skilled in the art of protecting her flock just like every other shepherd would have been. Her real struggle as indicated in Genesis 29 was the other shepherds at the well. I am sure there were men there with much smaller flocks. This did not sit well with them. Men measure so many things by size where as women do have a tendency to measure by worth or value. When we walk by sight and not by faith we often miss the true nature of God. Solomon exhorted every shepherd leader in Proverbs 27:23, Be diligent to know the state of thy flocks, and look well to your herds. Rachel proved herself a skillful shepherdess and was diligent in making sure the flock was well fed and well watered. Rachel also knew that Jacob had a great destiny.

She was a discerner of the family destiny. After all she bore Joseph the son who saved the seed from destruction. God truly blessed her.

As we leave Genesis we can see three very clear accounts of God using women as rulers and leaders. They were involved in creation, ruling, reigning, and giving birth to Kings. They of course are not leading in a church setting but they are the co-founders of the faith we all follow today. Think about that? These three women played significant roles in bringing God's plan to fulfillment in the earth.

Chapter 3

PROMENIENT WOMEN: THE OLD TESTAMENT

As we continue to move through the scriptures we come to the book of the Exodus. Stephen the first recorded martyr of the early church calls the deliverance of the Israelites from Egypt a type of the "church in the wilderness" Acts 7:38. Church of course in the Greek, means a group of called out ones.

THE PROPHETESS MIRIAM

As we look at the church in the wilderness we must acknowledge who is in leadership. Moses, Aaron, and Miriam are not only brothers and sister but they are all mouthpieces for the Lord. Of course, Moses is known as speaking the very words of God, and God himself calls Moses the greatest prophet of whom he communes with on a face to face level.

And he said, hear now my words: "If there is a prophet among you, I the Lord will make myself known to him in a vision and I will speak to him in a dream, not so my servant Moses, who is faithful in all my house. With him I will speak mouth to mouth even apparently, and not in dark speeches" Numbers 12:6-8a

Aaron, was Moses mouthpiece as they stood before Pharaoh, (per Moses request) Exodus 4:13-16.

Miriam plays a unique role in the deliverance of Israel. She was there at Moses drawing forth from the waters of the Nile. It was her suggestion to have her very own mother nurse the baby for Pharaoh's daughter. What a word of wisdom.

Exodus 2: 1-10 "And there went a man of the house of Levi, and took to wife a daughter of Levi. And the woman conceived and bare a son: and when she saw him that he was a goodly child, she hid him for three months. And when she could not any longer hide him, she took for him an ark of bulrushes, and daubed it with slime and with pitch and put the child in it: and she laid it in the flags by the river's bank. And his SISTER stood afar off to see what would become of the child. And the daughter of Pharaoh came down to wash herself at the river; and her maidens walked along by the river's side: and when she saw the ark among the flags she sent her maidens to get it. And when she opened it she saw the child: and behold the babe wept. And she had compassion on him, and said, This is one of the Hebrews' children. Then his SISTER said, Shall I go and call a nurse of the Hebrew women, that she may nurse the child for you? And Pharaoh's daughter said to her, Go. The maid went and called the child's mother." Exodus 2:1-10

Words of wisdom and knowledge often accompany the prophetic. I do not believe that her mother told her to do such an act. They had no idea what would happen and how Pharaoh's daughter would respond but were moved by faith that God would favor the child. In fact, Miriam gave Moses his first appearing at the house of Pharaoh. She hand delivered him at the right age to Pharaoh's daughter for his upbringing in the palace. Miriam acted with incredible wisdom for such a young girl.

When Pharaoh's army was destroyed she took the tambourine and began to lead the women in dance and song. According to the scripture she was an established prophetess.

AND MIRIAM THE PROPHETESS... Exodus 15:20

In Exodus 15 we have the record of the song of Moses and Miriam. Miriam is singing and dancing and leading the women. She was clearly a mouthpiece for the Lord. People followed her leadership.

Her only recorded failure before the Lord and the church dealt with her speaking. She criticized the marriage of Moses and it angered God. Perhaps she felt slighted by Moses in some way and it led to a bitter heart. Or maybe she had the big sister syndrome: we can only speculate as to the reason she chose to be critical of Moses and his marriage. Nevertheless, she was healed and God did use her in the church. Sometimes what God does not say is as important as what He does say!

Although Miriam was not a part of the physical priesthood as that was reserved for men under the Old Covenant, she was a VOICE; she had a speaking gift. This gift of prophecy is the one that is carried over into the New Testament and is a source of contention among churches and ministries today. Particularly whether or not women can speak, preach, teach, or should they simply be silent? We will discover that according to the Bible it has never been God's intention for women to be silent any more than for men to be silent in the church.

Miriam spoke out and sang in the church of the Old Testament. Notice that the prayer ministry was reserved for the men. Isn't that ironic? In the church today it seems that mostly women are regulated to intercessory prayer, yet the greatest intercessors of the Old Testament were men. Abraham, Jacob, Moses, Elijah are known for their intercession as much as their offices and their miracles. I wonder where the praying men are.

To sum up Miriam's ministry, she acted in a word of wisdom that saved Moses life early on and also moved prophetically in the church, having a speaking role before the people.

WOMEN AND THE LAW

DAUGHTERS of ZELOPHEHAD the first female LAW FIRM

Another interesting case of women taking a leadership role is found in Numbers 27:1-11.

In this passage, five sisters the daughters of Zelophehad the descendant of Manasseh, the son of Joseph, (ruler of Egypt) approach Moses over the legal issue of their inheritance. They were Mahlah, Noah, Hoglah, Milcah, and Tirzah.... these women are not your usual set of sisters. They obviously had had many discussions about the inheritance laws of Israel. The inheritance was a man's job and a man's lot. As they laid their case before Moses he went to God and God said to listen to them. They, by their leadership, changed the inheritance laws for many.

Although they are not called leaders in the sense that we view leaders, they did take initiative to change a cultural bias. INITIATION is one of the greatest traits of leaders. They dared to enter an area that was reserved for men, the law. The making, giving, writing and execution of laws were reserved for the men. These ladies had amazing courage to approach the door to the tent of meeting where only the men dwell. Just as the prophetic often confronts the injustices of the culture, these ladies while not labeled prophets certainly had the courage to seek justice.

We can see God blessing their counsel in an age and time when women were not heard. These sisters brought the church in the wilderness closer to being a culture of grace and honor for all people regardless of gender.

Unity is to be sought by everyone in the church but often ladies will unite much quicker than men. Women have that sense of wanting to be together and seek to create a welcoming environment much more often than men.

BOOKS OF KINGS AND CHRONICLES:

HULDAH the PROPHETESS

There was a prophetess Huldah whom King Josiah sent his servants to inquire of the Lord. The story is recorded in II Kings 22:14 and II Chronicles 34:22. Here it says she was the wife of a man whose father was the keeper of the Kings wardrobe and that she dwelt in the college. College here in the Hebrew means second quarter of the city. Her dwelling was obviously one of importance and men knew the exact location. We have no record of her prophesying anywhere else in scripture but due to the fact that King Josiah sent for her confirmation of the book of the law that he discovered seems to indicate that she held a prominent position at that time. Her prophetic gift was acknowledged, and sought out by the King. She interpreted the meaning and prominence of the book of Deuteronomy to Josiah as well as the high priest and Josiah's staff. To speak prophetically to the King and to be sought out by him is leadership at the highest level: on par with Isaiah, Jeremiah, and other great prophets of the Old Testament. Kings often had counsels. David was often guided by Ahithiphel, a famous counselor. Huldah is the only Old Testament woman mentioned to be sought out by a King.

JUDGES

DEBORAH the JUDGE

Women in today's culture can be found in every leadership role in society. Doctors, lawyers, entrepreneur's, truck drivers, police officers, and of course judges; the church must ask itself why so much confusion and limitation over the role of women as elders, pastor's, evangelist, prophets and teachers?

I remember once many years ago going to hear a woman whose fame was somewhat renowned in the church world. Her books are read by the brightest and best minds, her radio program was heard extensively. The conference I attended had her stuck in one of the lesser rooms while the main speaker, the man of power for the hour held the large auditorium. Well, to everyone's surprise the host center had to open up extensions in the ballroom area as so many people came to hear this lady speak. It was indeed a great session about the forgiveness of God.

I was deeply saddened later when I contacted her ministry to discuss having her come to our church for a weekend seminar and of course ending with her speaking on Sunday morning. I was told by her husband that she would be allowed to do Sunday School but that she could not ever stand behind a pulpit. I held my composure, gave my sincere thanks and hung up the phone. His response was such a telling attitude of what is wrong and overly simplistic about the church. For centuries the question of a women's role has been argued over with intense passion. If this woman could address a few thousand people in a convention hall where Christians (the church) were gathered, why not in another building? Jesus told us to preach a message to all men, not set up rules for a piece of wood or class called a pulpit. I guess man made rules make us feel secure about the things we fear.

Now on to Deborah: This woman of God bursts on the scene at a time of national crisis in Israel. There was no leadership, male or female. In Judges Chapters 4 & 5 we have her story. She sat under a palm tree and judged the nation with prophetic insight. She was a ruler, leader, and prophetess. She was obviously a very wise woman as well. Barrack, the designated leader was afraid and would only go to war if she were with him. She had a prophetic word that when Barrack went up to battle that the Lord would deliver Sisera the captain of the Canaanite army into the hands of a woman. He obeyed her wise counsel and led the way. During the battle Sisera escaped on foot. Exhausted and weary he wound up at the tent door of one named Heber (a descendant of Moses father in law). He was greeted by his wife Ja-el. He asked for water and she gave him milk. As he slept she took a nail (tent peg) and drove it through his temple fastening it to the ground. She then beheaded him! Just as Deborah prophesied, the Lord gave the ultimate victory into the hand of a woman. Ja-el demonstrated a warrior spirit and so opposite of the feminine nature created a ghastly act of murder during battle.

After this great battle Deborah sang along with Barrack about the victories of the Lord and the defeat of his enemies. She was unequivocally the leader of the nation. Spiritually, governmentally, and just as great generals ride into battle she rode with the guys.

ABIGAIL the WISE WIFE

You cannot really discuss women in a thorough way unless you discuss women in relationship to the home. Paul gives a lot of instruction about a woman's role in the family and marriage relationship.

Perhaps the biggest issue along with women in ministry has been the issue of women in regards to SUBMISSION. Much heartache has resulted from the application of that word without the true spirit of Christ in the church. Countless women have been counseled to stay in physically abusive relationships, sexual practices of the most Cannite (depraved nature). Women have lost inheritances and fortunes, squandered by irresponsible men. Often these men have held positions of leadership in the church such as deacons, elders, Pastor, evangelist…well you get the picture.

Submission has been accepted in some circles of the church world as eternal doctrine most sacred and holy! However the passages dealing with submission have been mostly misquoted and applied in all sorts of situations to sanction behavior that is certainly less than our role model, the Lord Jesus Christ.

Abigail was married to a man who was himself a bit void of understanding in relationship to certain social protocol.

"Now the name of the man was Nabal; and the name of his wife was Abigail; and she was a woman of good understanding, and of a beautiful countenance: by the man was churlish and evil in his doings; and he was of the house of Caleb." I Samuel 25:3

The Bible says he was churlish; this is the only time this word is used in scripture. It means to be cruel, grievous, hard hearted, obstinate, rough, stubborn, and stiff-necked. As you can see he was obviously a difficult man to live with. Being a Pastor you are often called for marriage counseling. Many times I have met churlish men. They have enough of their "own religion", man made to suit them and they expect the good wife to comply. They refuse to tithe, to serve, to help out and often they put such emotional pressure on their wives that they will finally drop out of church altogether in the name of submission to my husband. Paul's letters are often quoted to substantiate such carnal behavior. Many Pastors's fail to apprehend Paul's words to Christian marriages and consequently fail to challenge the man. Submission is not a women's role in the home and marriage. Submission is an attitude of preferring your mate, male or female in a sense of respect and value.

> The Bible does actually say: "Wives, submit yourselves unto
> your husbands as unto the Lord." Ephesians 5:22

This Chapter has been so misused to propagate a lifestyle of emotional, mental, and physical poverty beyond human reasoning. This entire chapter is giving us as men the responsibility to treat our wives as Christ treats the church. It is interesting that this chapter also does not tell the wife to love her husband but it does tell husbands to love their wives. This is leadership par-excellence as a Christian man should follow the example of Christ in every aspect.

Jesus did not wait for us to submit to his love before he loved us. Because he loved us we submitted. In counseling we often leave off the Christ role for the male and come down heavy on a woman who is a bit frustrated with a man who is not fulfilling his conjugal duties in many respects. SUBMITTING YOURSELVES ONE TO ANOTHER IN THE FEAR OF GOD, Ephesians 5:21, this is the very heart of what Paul is teaching to believers in regards to a Christian marriage.

Now back to Abigail. David approaches Nabal for some help during a stressful time. Because her husband is selfish and undiscerning of authority even that of the king…he refuses to help David and his men and as a result David is going to kill him. David was anything but churlish. He walked in submission to authority even bad authority. He recognized things most men never see. He understood his relationship with God and his calling and that made all the difference.

Abigail who was wise and submitted averts the disaster by ignoring her husband and doing the right thing. Thank God she did or perhaps she would have lost her own life as well. Abigail not only saved her husband but later is taken as one of David's wives. This was probably the highest honor a lady could have had during her day. If she would have been in some of our churches she would have been instructed to "submit" to Nabal and God will bless her. If she had she would have lost her life.

I realize this is sacred cow territory and we have a long way to go in some circles but thank God for wives who do know how to submit to God and trust him even if it means disagreeing with her husband and perhaps saving the family home from foreclosure, or saving herself from years of physical abuse, or the kids if there are any involved. Abigail is a role model for us to study. She acted out of character for her time and saved herself and her family from destruction. Nabal did die apparently of some type of stroke or heart failure but Abigail was a model wife even if she did disobey her husband.

ESTHER the QUEEN

Esther plays a very unique role as far as leadership. Here we see the incredible power of a women's influence over her husband. I think that this example is probably one of the most stunning in the Bible.

She goes against the culture norm and the law of the land and succeeds! How rare is that?

She finds a way to lead without being bossy or usurping her role. In fact her submission is a major key in her fulfilling the role to save the nation. She submits to her Uncle's wise counsel and rescues the nation from total annihilation. She does clash with at least one tradition that could cost her life!

She enters the courts of the King uninvited and unannounced. This was nothing short of blasphemous to the office of the King. We do not know for sure what Xerxes saw in her but we do know he extended his scepter to her. She found favor with the king. She used her POSITION to PETITION. Every leader knows the power of their position. If they do not they will not lead long. She exercises her position as wife to request a favor. It is granted and the rest is history as we know it today.

A man could not have done what she did. Why did God choose to use a woman to deliver a nation from annihilation? Sometimes God chooses the very thing we reject to deliver us. The deliverance does not happen unless we receive the one he has sent to deliver. So many men have perhaps missed a moment of God's grace because it appeared in a female body. We cannot receive the MESSAGE sometimes because we are so focused on the MESSANGER. God chooses who he wishes to speak and lead through, and many times in history, he has chosen a woman.

The late great Kathryn Kulhman said that God had chosen three men to carry the anointing of healing that she carried and they said no. With all due respect to late great Ms. Kulhman, God need not appear to settle for something less than what he wants. He wanted her and even if the other men she spoke of would have answered God's call to the healing and miracle ministry they would or could have never expressed it the way she did. I think God chose her specifically to humble many people whose trust is in the flesh.

God chose Esther not Ernest to deliver and who are we to argue and make pompous platitudes about why or who he has chosen.

Chapter 4

WOMEN IN THE NEW TESTAMENT

The New Testament is filled with many examples of women in leadership both secular and sacred. In fact, the New Testament is filled with much stronger and clearer examples of women in leadership roles in the church than the Old Testament.

When the Apostle Paul comes on the scene in ancient times the world has progressed tremendously as far as cultural advancement for women. The Roman Empire was at its height. Ephesus was a much a cosmopolitan city as New York or San Francisco. Corinth was a melting pot of the world and women were involved in many facets of society, art, leadership, and government.

Now, Paul gives an interesting message to the church at Corinth about church government when he says in:

> I Corinthians 12:27 "But you are the body of Christ and members of the part. And God appointed in the church first apostles,

second prophets, third teachers, then miracle workers, then gifts of healing, helpers, directors, and kinds of languages."

Now compare this with the passage to the church at Ephesus.

Ephesians 4:11-12 "It was he who gave some to be apostles, some to be prophets, some to be evangelist, and some to be pastor's and teachers, to prepare God's people for works of service so that the body of Christ may be built up..."

Paul is giving us the expressed will of the Father through the Holy Spirit as to how the church should be governed. We must allow the Bible to speak on its own authority. We should not try to water down the scriptures to fit our thinking. We must elevate our thinking to embrace the words of God.

By defining these governmental offices we can see that by definition of the word itself and the people named who fill these offices, that they do not exclude females. In other words the definitions are not GENDER driven. They are what they are and any person male or female can fit the definition. Let's examine each gift and see if there is a scriptural example to support a women operating in that gift.

APOSTLES

APOSTLE: Apostolos in the Greek. Meaning one sent with a message or orders. This word used by Paul was the only word that was not based in the previous canon of scripture. In other words apostle was a secular term used to describe a type of solider or government representative whose mission was to deliver the message of a sovereign. For example, an apostle of Rome was to go into conquered territory and not just enforce the Roman law but the mission of an apostle was to convert the MINDS of the people to Roman culture. Apostles had full power, legally, militarily, and educationally to enforce the conversion of the populace to the Roman way. The heart of apostleship is soul conversion. We do know that there were no women serving in the Roman army in this capacity. This contributes to the idea of a male only position.

Another contribution I am sure is that of Jesus and the 12 Apostles of the Lamb. No ladies represented here and rightly so due to cultural norms of the day. Women and men unless married did not travel together or for that fact do much of anything together. It appears that according to culture and military service that women would be excluded from this role.

Paul in recounting Christ post-resurrection appearances states in I Corinthians 15:5 that Jesus appeared to the 12 apostles and in that same chapter verse 7 he says that later he appeared to all the apostles. So, we can see that even during Jesus ministry there were other apostles than the 12. Who were they? **By stating that there were other apostles, Paul let's us know that it was accepted during the early church that there were more than just the 12 men Jesus chose. Who were the others?**

We know that Paul was one. Barnabas is mentioned in Acts 14:14 along with Paul. Others are mentioned in the book of Acts on several occasions. Paul addresses Andronicus and Junia in his greeting to the Roman Christians. He even mentions the fact that they were apostles before him. Romans 16:7.

Paul makes an interesting statement in the letter to the Galatians as he is describing his journey right after his conversion. He says that he did not go up to Jerusalem to those who were apostles before me but went into Arabia and Damascus. Then he makes his way to Jerusalem and stays with Peter for fifteen days. Then he says he did not see any of the apostles except James the brother of Christ. Again, this alludes to other apostles than the 12. (Galatians 1:19)

Although Jesus did not choose a woman to travel with him (I think this is based on the practicum and logistics of such a situation: just as women did not learn to read and write, they most likely traveled little as well.) We do however see Mary of Magdala, Joanna, Mary the mother of Jesus, Mary the mother of James, wife of Alphaeus, and Salome, mother of James and John and wife of Zebedee, were women who TRAVELED and followed Jesus ministry albeit not living with the men of course.

Dr. Luke records this for us:

> Luke 8: 1-3 "And it came about soon afterwards, the He began going from one city and village to another, proclaiming and preaching the kingdom of God; and the twelve were with Him, and also some WOMEN who had been healed of evil spirits and sicknesses: Mary who was called Magdalene, from whom seven demons had gone out, and Joanna the wife of Chuza,

Herod's steward, and Susanna, and many others who were con-
tributing to their support out of their private means."

WOMEN WERE AN INTREGAL PART OF JESUS MINISTRY

We have to ask the question, is there any woman called by name in scripture that is referred to or directly addressed as an apostle? Paul mentions Junia
in Romans 16:8 as an apostle before him. Junia is a common Latin woman's
name. Junis is the male counterpart, as Priscus is the male counterpart to Prisca.
Through the centuries early church leaders translated Junia as a womans name.
Several clear references are as follows:

> *Origen, who was a church father and lived towards the end of
> the second century, assumed Junia was a woman. He wrote in
> his Epistolam ad Romanos Commentariorum 10, 26: 39.
> *John Chrysostrom, living in the fourth century praised her:
> "Oh how great is the devotion of this woman that she should be
> even counted worthy of the appellation of Apostle! (Homily on
> the Epistle of St. Paul to the Romans XXXI)

Other commentators such as Jerome considered Junia a woman. There has
been hair-splitting and straining at a gnat to swallow a camel with the interpretation of this name for centuries. But it is safe to say that she and Andronicus
helped lay the foundation for the churches at Rome and they were notable fig-
ures held in the highest of esteem among those Paul considered colleagues.

I realize that other prominent Bible Leaders have come to interpret Junia as a man. We are all entitled to our interpretation but I wonder when exactly did the words of Origen and Chrysostrom became translated now to mean a man? These early church fathers seem to be a little older than most of our modern scholars and perhaps relied upon a more closer interpretation of Junia based upon the passed down knowledge of those who lived closer to the century of the birthing of the church in the book of Acts.

I believe that if one woman was named in this position there had to be others operating in this gift as well. I am not a church historian by any means but I am sure that other women have held positions of authority over men in a leadership role.

In our modern life time we have seen women of Apostolic stature and gifting. Amiee Simple McPherson who is the founder of the Four Square denomination. She was billed as an evangelist/pastor but this woman flowed in an apostolic anointing that is affecting the world today.

Other women known affectionately as missionaries were indeed apostles. Amy Carmichael–whose endeavors in India changed a barbaric culture. Catherine Booth co-founder of the Salvation Army. Ann Lee the founder of the Shaker movement. These women and many others like them had a clear call and experience with Jesus Christ just as real as any man. They not only brought the church to a new level of spirituality but impacted the culture and changed society in many ways. Men had ceased to be called apostles as well until the recent restoration of this office in the church. The church now freely uses a term that would have horrified many believers a few centuries ago, since there could only be the original twelve. How dare us to take such a title to ourselves!

But the power of PRESENT DAY TRUTH as the apostle Peter said, is ever moving the church forward to the soon coming of our wonderful King!

PROPHETS

PROPHET: someone who receives and speaks forth a message from God.

In the birth of Christ we see prophets, kings, and wise men. There was a woman prophetess named Anna who appeared at the right moment to bless Jesus at his eight day dedication in the temple.

> "And there was one Anna, a prophetess, the daughter of Phaneul, of the tribe of Asher: she was of a great age, and had lived with her husband seven years from her virginity; And she was a widow of about four-score and four years, (84) which departed not from the temple, but served God with fastings and prayers night and day." Luke 2:36

That there were women prophets in the New Testament ministry of the church is first given credence through and Old Testament prophet name Joel.

> "And it shall come to pass afterward that I will pour out my spirit upon all flesh; and your sons and DAUGHTERS shall prophesy, your old men will dream dreams, and your young men will see visions. And also upon the servants and upon the

HANDMAIDS in those days I will pour out my spirit." Joel 2:28.29

Paul while instructing those flowing in the gifts at Corinth does not restrict them to a certain GENDER but to an orderly DEMONSTRATION that all may learn and grow.

"And the next day we that were of Paul's company departed, and came unto Caesarea: and we entered into the house of Philip the evangelist, which was one of the seven; and abode with him. And the same man had four daughters, virgins, who did prophesy. Acts 21:8, 9.

All though these girls are not called prophets we see the fulfillment again of Joel's prophesy about women prophesying.

TEACHERS

In the Old Testament Solomon in writing of the Proverbs describes wisdom as a woman. Hence the aspect of teaching.

TEACHER: one who instructs in knowledge.

Priscilla, who was at Ephesus during Paul's ministry, was an able teacher.

> Acts 18:26 "Having heard (Apollos), Priscilla and Aquila took him aside and more accurately expounded to him the way of God."

The Greek word for expounding is Ektithemai, and it means: expound, to set forth, declare, exhibit publicly, and explain by means of abstraction.

In the letter to Titus, Paul mentions the aged women.

> Titus 2:3 "The aged women likewise, that they be in behavior as becometh holiness, not false accusers, not given to much wine, TEACHERS of good things."

The word for old is presbutis and is best translated female elder. Paul calls them teachers of the good. These women of Crete were instructed by Paul to use their teaching ability to serve the church, just as a male leader, be it Bishop or Apostle or Pastor would do so.

EVANGELIST

EVANGELIST: from evangel in the Greek to proclaim good news!

The New Testament does not call any women evangelist. It list only one man called by this title that was Philip. Acts 21:8.

Timothy is exhorted by Paul to do the work on an evangelist in II Timothy 4:5.

However the role of an evangelist is to tell the good news of Jesus Christ. We see several women being used by God in the New Testament to do just that.

The fruit of an evangelist as judged by Phillip is the conversion of a group or mass of people or an entire city.

In the gospel of John chapter 4 we have the story of the Samaritan women at the well. It is interesting that she was able to rally a large part of the city to come and see Jesus and in verse 39 it states that MANY of the Samartians of that city believed on him for the work of the woman (HE TOLD ME ALL THAT I EVER DID).

Like Phillips outreach many in the city believed. Philip did have miracles but Jesus word of knowledge was a miracle that impacted the women thus enabling her to tell of his greatness and see a large part of her town converted to Christ.

And of course there is Mary at the Resurrection. If evangelists tell the good news then God chose a woman to be the first to convey the greatest miracle in history to the apostles. We know in all four gospel records that Jesus appeared to the women first. He did not tell them to keep quiet about it. He could have since he often instructed people who had received miracles to remain quiet about it. Instead he specifically told them to go and tell the Apostles and Peter that he had risen. His greatest miracle ever was given first utterance by women

PASTORS

PASTOR: One, who in modern terms oversees a church, cares for people, like a shepherd in the Old Testament.

There is no New Testament record of a woman being called a Pastor. Neither is the term used to describe a man.

The only person called Pastor (poimen) is JESUS.

We do however see many women named as overseers. The Elect Lady, the Elect Sister, Phoebe, Euodia, Syntyche, Prisca, Stephana, Tryphaena, Tryphosa, Chole, Lydia, Nympha, and Apphia.

In II John 1:1, 5 he refers to the elect lady. In the Greek (Kuria) is the feminine of (Kurios), which means a person who owns an estate and is free and not subject to guardians and trustees. The kurios is the guardian, master of the house, or a head of the family. In its simplest form it means one who has authority. The elect lady was the one in charge and she had been chosen by God to be in that position according to John. The last verse of this epistle John calls to our attention an elect sister as well.

Notice that in Romans 16:13 Rufus is referred to as elect. "Elect persons in the New Testament can and do refer to clergy such as presbyters, bishops, deacons, and widows." We can conclude that this was probably a house church since most New Testament churches met in homes.

A few examples of churches meeting in the houses of women are:

Chloe (I Cor.1:11)

Lydia (Acts 16:40)

The Mother of John Mark (Acts 12:12)

Nympha (Col 4:15)

Philemon, Apphia, and Archippus (Philemon 1-2)

Prisca and Aquila (Romans 16:3-5)

Lydia played an important role in the Philippian Church. She was not only a church leader but business woman as well. Her fabric or dye company was successful and she was honored to serve the apostles in her home. She led the prayer meeting as well.

Phoebe is praised by Paul the apostle as a minister and leader. Paul says she was the leader of the church at Cenchreae. The word used by Paul to describe her is diakonons and is literally translated servant. The word was used in the church to describe one who ministers the word of God for the equipping of the saints. Another use was translated to mean the servant of a sovereign, or one who assist the sovereign in implementing and delivering orders. Finally it is used to signify a person who meets the physical needs of another, be they food, drink, shelter, or clothing.

Phoebe according to Paul is not only a minister but one who should be welcomed and considered worthy by the saints at Rome and given the assistance she needs. He tells us that she has been a succorer (prostatis) over many and even Paul himself. This word is used to describe on who helps in ruling. It is obvious that Phoebe is a woman who is set over others, or one who stands before. No other person in the New Testament is called a prostatis. Phoebe is an excellent and commendable example of a woman being set over a man. Even the great apostle Paul views her over himself at some capacity, during some portion of his ministry.

Paul also uses the term co-workers to describe other prominent women in ministry. He calls, Euodia and Syntyche, Tryphaena and Tryphosa his workers. Co-worker comes from two words meaning to work together. It can signify is certain cases, a helper, but Paul uses the genitive case of the word which means, "a person of the same trade," a colleague. Paul refers to apostles, prophets, evangelist, and teachers as co-workers together in this glorious goal.

Chapter 5

PAUL'S VIEW OF
WOMEN IN MINSISTRY

aving examined the New Testament examples of women in every
role of leadership, we have to turn our attention to the two passages of the New Testament that seem to exclude women from ministering the
word of God in the area of preaching, teaching or governing over men.

I find it amazing that the very Apostle and Champion of women in ministry
Paul himself is today used to disqualify women from the pulpit. We will look at
the two passages most often used and see how they line up with Paul's lifestyle
as well as his teaching about women leaders.

Our first one reads:

> "I suffer not a woman to teach, nor usurp authority over the
> man but to be in silence. I Timothy 2:11-12

This verse comes at the end of an exhortation by Paul concerning prayer.
If you go back to the beginning of the chapter he is speaking about the first

priority of the believer is to pray and he instructs them how to pray and who to pray for. He moves in verse 8 to the posture of men in prayer, lifting holy hands and then transitions to women that they are to have a modest apparel and sobriety of spirit. He then goes on to say that women should learn in silence. Perhaps the women here that were in Timothy's church had a habit of speaking out in prayer service? Perhaps they had even led some prayers that were not theologically correct? Perhaps they were praying to angels as others had done and had to be corrected. I believe this verse of silence is in relationship to prayer. As I stated earlier the great intercessors of the Bible were mostly men. Perhaps a few women were moving in that direction and it was shaking up the culture of the men leading in prayer? We really do not know but one thing we can know for sure is that Paul would never think of not using women in a teaching, preaching and leading role. I say that based upon his lifestyle. He welcomed women and lifted them up and upheld their leadership in the church at the time.

Come to think of it, who can learn while talking? No one. He also adds that he does not allow a woman to teach. This is most interesting given the record of his praise for Priscilla who taught Apollos a more excellent way. He also instructs the elder women at Crete to teach. So, is he really making a blanket statement about women teaching in any of his churches at any time? The women he praised in the house church roles all had to have some ability to instruct others in the faith. (TEACH)

Next he says do not usurp authority. To usurp means to take something that is not given to you. Neither a woman nor a man should attempt to take spiritual authority that is not given them. Paul gives Phoebe authority over himself and he gives respect for women in authority calling them by name and compelling other leaders and followers to respect them. If he really meant that no woman should be in authority over a man ever, or that they should not teach then I am sure his epistles to the churches would have spent more time straitening out the mess of having women leaders. Can we put this in perspective? I think Paul was addressing an issue affecting that church and no other, like he did in most of his letters.

One last thought, not to be a literalist, but he does not say, "You shall not allow a woman to preach?" Every church leader knows there is a difference between preaching and teaching. He does not say, "You shall not allow a woman to prophesy, or to evangelize." If Paul truly meant to exclude women from ministry then he was indeed a hypocrite.

The next troubling passage that is used reads as follows:

"Let your women keep silence in the churches: for it is not permitted unto them to speak: but they are commanded to be under obedience, as also says the law. And if they learn anything, let them ask their husbands at home: for it is a shame for women to speak in church. WHAT, did the word of God originate with you?" I Corinthians 14:34-36

This seems to be the nail in the coffin for most men who struggle with a women preaching and teaching. I mean, here it is in black and white! Well, Paul's style of writing was often question and answer. He also uses a bit of satire often in dealing with the lack of spiritual understanding in the church and the culture around him. Also, I am sure you are aware that the Bible was not written in Chapter and verse form. The New Testament Epistles were letters without numerical separation of thoughts that we read today. If you take the time to read the letters without dividing them into chapters and verses you may find the meaning of some well cherished phrases suddenly become a little different than there commonly held interpretations. I believe this passage is just such an incident. The Corinthian church obviously held some cherished ideas of a woman's role in their churches. Paul simply writes out their idea and with a bit of satire and strong expression he challenges this belief. By stating their belief and using the simple word WHAT!, he changes the entire previous expression by questioning it.

I think Paul is shocked at the mindset of the Corinthians. It appears from his rhetorical answer that he is challenging what they are doing, not setting down a rule for all to follow. Paul is not confirming this attitude quiet the contrary he is a bit aghast at this pompous mindset. He says what are you saying? Do you think you have a monopoly on the word of God? Did God consult you and decide you were the ones with true revelation? Did God's laws originate with you?

So we can see that Paul was not telling the Corinthians to treat their women this way. If he was, then again, he was a hypocrite since he never treated women in this manner in his own ministry and travels. He affirmed and promoted them which are quiet the opposite.

Chapter 6

Women Leaders in the Church Culture

*I*n the church since the 1900's we have seen great women leaders such as Amiee Semple McPherson, of Pentecostal Fame. Kathern Khulman brought to the church perhaps one the most amazing healing ministries of this century. Many great Pentecostal women have arisen since the 1960's, Dr. Fuschia Pickett, Marilyn Hickey, Joyce Meyer, Pastor Ann Gimmenez, and Cindy Jacobs a prophetess/apostle. And of course the many women (too numerous to name in this small booklet) who co-pastor with their husbands and run mega churches all across our nation.

Mother Teresa of the Catholic Church and many other Nuns who have done amazing things yet not received as much recognition, as she.

Episcopal/Charismatic leaders like LeAnn Payne, and others. Evangeline Booth co-founder of the Salvation Army perhaps the most influential Christian group to be still going after over 100 years of dedicated soul winning and helping the poor.

The Evangelical stream has produced many great women leaders such as Henrietta Mears, Kay Arthur, Ruth Graham Lotz, Elizabeth Elliot, and Amy Carmichael. These women have and (those that have gone on to glory), still do bring to the church a refreshing and exciting presence of God.

The Psalmist David said, "The streams make glad the city of God." We see women in every major stream of the spirit in the church today.

In trying to honor God's Word, we have perhaps refused to look at the obvious as it is played out in church culture and the world around us. We have often chosen what I call TRADITIONAL COMMENTARY CULTURE over truth. By this I mean, the words of some truly great thinkers have taken the place of our own thoughts and imprisoned us to think no more since we have a plausible answer. Therefore, we no longer question what we believe. We have done this not only with women but with worship, with giving, with dress, with evangelism, with money, and in reaching the next generation. It is time for us to awaken to the fact that women are capable and called by God to hold church offices and to possess spiritual gifting.

Chapter 7

Women in the Secular Culture

omen in society have seemed to be received in a more welcome way although there is still much room for improvement. The list of secular world leaders is impressive. Margaret Thatcher the first women Prime Minister of England, Golda Meir the leader of the Nation of Israel, Indria Gandhi, the President of India the second largest nation on earth, Queen Elizabeth celebrating her 60th diamond jubilee, Angelia Merkel the Chancellor of Germany, Meg Ryan, the CEO of E-Bay, and many other women who today lead large corporations. These women carry the responsibilities traditionally attributed to men. We cannot deny that all through history women have excelled in culture in every area, from government, to the arts, to science, medicine, and literature.

Women were created in the image of God just like men were. In most cultures today where women are oppressed we see financial and social poverty. Not all mind you, but in quiet a few. I believe that in devaluing God's creation we open the door for less than what he has intended for us. This is true not only with the women question but other areas in the church world.

The youth for example, being regulated to second tier status when the Biblical record is clear that most leaders in the Bible were quiet young when they made history with God. The gifts of the spirit, trying to always regulate how and when the Holy Spirit can move in a service or judging the experience of a believer. Regulating, the Holy Spirit to a few we like to call mystics.

The devaluing of women has always kept the human race in a less than stellar destiny that God has prepared us for. I pray that we will all begin to rethink our positions on many subjects we have held near and dear, locked in the box of our comfortable religion and smugly holding the key. The keys of the kingdom Christ spoke of were more than knowledge. Knowledge without experience is a travesty waiting to happen.

May we realize God only limited himself to a box one time. In the Tabernacle of Moses, he made the Ark of the Covenant and said his glory would dwell there over the mercy seat. When Christ died and rose again, this box became big enough to fill heaven and earth with his glory. Perhaps we should rethink our ideas of God in a cultural sense, and dare to see how big he truly is!

Chapter 8

Kingdom Living

I do believe that there are differences between men and women. I believe that both sexes have strengths and weakness that the other needs.

Paul does say in Galatians 3:28 that in Christ we are neither male nor female, Jew nor Greek, bond nor free...he begins in verse 26 of this chapter stating that we are all sons of God. He uses a masculine term. I think Paul is trying to get us to emphasize relationship with God and not perceived gender or cultural roles. Like the church in the wilderness the laws were given to emphasize sonship and relationship with God as opposed to the relationship of slavery.

Those dear saints by faith under the old covenant never perceived their relationship with God but held fast to the false rule of generational slavery their hearts had labored under for over 400 years.

In my 30 plus years of ministry I have seen terrible and terrific leaders both male and female: good male pastors and bad male pastors, good women pastors and bad women pastors etc. Gifting in human beings has had stellar results both male and female, as well as tragedy by both sexes.

We must emphasize the Kingdom of God and not the cultural disqualifications of what we call ministry. This is hard to hear and harder yet to live. When you study the gospels and you see the emphasis of Christ on the Kingdom of God please notice that the parables he taught and the supernatural he displayed was never focused by him to restrict women. Women heard him preach, women received healing, women gave money, women evangelized for Him.

We are witnessing in American culture right now the systematic destruction of sexual differences in the name of equality or equal rights. Paul laid out a strong case against tampering with the natural creation of God in relationship to men and women:

"For although they knew God, they neither glorified him as God nor gave thanks to him, but their thinking became futile and their foolish hearts were darkened. Although they claimed to be wise they became fools and exchanged the glory of the immortal God for images made to look like mortal man and birds and animals and reptiles." Romans 1:22-25.

We are astute enough to see the slow disintegration of cultural to its lowest forms of depravity when people willfully neglect the knowledge of God. I am not trying to equalize men and women and tear down any distinctions. The distinctions are quiet noticeable to all and no matter how many legislative moves are made to try and make us sexless (neither male nor female) it will not change the creation of man as God has clearly designed it. There are roles that men and women have carried throughout the history of the human race and some of those roles are best fulfilled by men and other roles women will always be responsible for and do much better than men. I am simply stating the obvious life of the Holy Spirit in the church as He chooses to whom He gives gifts and offices too.

WE ARE NOT ALLOWED TO DISTRIBUTE THE GIFTS OF THE HOLY SPIRIT NOR ARE WE ALLOWED TO CHOSE WHOM HE DECIDES TO CALL INTO A CERTAIN MINISTRY.

He often chooses vessels that we simply cannot seem to accept. We have to constantly check our pride and purpose in serving the Lord and advancing his will on the earth. The women question will not go away but there is a remnant who understands the need for Kingdom living. May we all continually be seekers of His Kingdom and His righteousness, not our church structures and our cultural rules in regards to the Presence of the Holy Spirit in the church.

The scriptures which are the standard for all believers do indicate the role of women in the church for every gifting and office. We must decide whether we will hold fast to treasured tradition or be open to an expression of God as old as the Garden of Eden itself.

This book is lovingly dedicated to Lucie:

A Proverbs 31 women in every sense of the word.

PROVERBS 31:10-31

"A wife of noble character who can find? She is worth far more than rubies. Her husband has full confidence in her and lacks nothing of value. She brings him good, not harm, all the days of her life. She selects wool and flax and works with eager hands. She is like the merchant ships, bringing her food from afar. She gets up while it is still night; she provides food for her family and portions for her female servants. She considers a field and buys it; out of her earnings she plants a vineyard. She sets about her work vigorously; her arms are strong for her tasks. She sees that her trading is profitable, and her lamp does not go out at night. In her hand she holds the distaff and grasps the spindle with her fingers. She opens her arms to the poor and extends her hands to the needy. When it snows, she has no fear for her household; for all of them are clothed in scarlet. She makes coverings for her bed; she is clothed in fine linen and purple. Her husband is respected at the city gate, where he takes his seat among the elders of the land. She makes linen garments and sells them, and supplies the merchants with sashes. She is clothed with strength and dignity; she can laugh at the days to come. She speaks with wisdom, and faithful instruction is on her tongue. She watches over the affairs of her household and does not eat the bread of idleness. Her children arise and call her blessed; her husband also praises her; many women do noble things, but you surpass them all! Charm is deceptive and beauty is fleeting; but a woman who fears the Lord is to be praised. Honor her for all that her hands have done, and let her works bring her praise at the city gate."

CPSIA information can be obtained at www.ICGtesting.com
Printed in the USA
BVOW08s1625081114

374199BV00004B/5/P

9 781498 407014